Unpacking yourself !

Dhamini Kandhavel

BookLeaf Publishing
India | USA | UK

Presentation by *BookLeaf Publishing*

Web: www.bookleafpub.com

E-mail: info@bookleafpub.com

ISBN: 9789363300637

First edition 2024

"To the Little Star,

Twinkling on each page!"

ACKNOWLEDGEMENT

Writing a book is indeed a journey of the heart, mind, and soul—a journey, a gift of reflection and discovery, that could not have come to life without the support and encouragement of those who walked alongside me.

First and foremost, I offer my deepest gratitude to God, my first mentor and ever-present guide. Your divine wisdom has illuminated my path, making every word written a testament to your unwavering support.

To my beloved parents, my appa Kandhavel and my dear amma, Umarani, your unconditional love, wisdom, and strength have been the bedrock upon which I have built my dreams and have shaped me into the person I am today.

To my dear husband, Rajarajan, you are my greatest support and cheerleader. Your unwavering encouragement, patience, and belief in my dreams are my rock. Thank you for standing by my side throughout this journey and for being the "Yoyo" in my life.

I am profoundly grateful to Bookleaf Publishing for believing in my vision and assisting in bringing this book to life with such dedication.

To my cherished grandparents, my supportive in-laws, my dear thatha and aaya, and my beloved mams, atthai, and sissy, who shaped my childhood; to all my uncles, aunts, cousins, family, friends, well-wishers, and peers, especially my mentor and his beloved family—your unwavering support, encouragement, and appreciation have been my greatest strength and have deeply enriched my journey.

I also dedicate this book to Karthikrajan, our beloved friend, who will forever live in our hearts. Designing the front cover myself was a joy, and I am grateful he chose, liked, and appreciated it. I hope this book shines even brighter with his blessings from above.

To you, the readers who have embarked on this journey with me, thank you for choosing my book. This book is as much yours as it is mine.

Lastly, I thank the universe for the inspiration that flows through every word of this book.

It is my hope that 'Unpacking Yourself' serves as a mirror and a guide, illuminating the path to the little star within each of us.

With deepest appreciation,
Dhamini Kandhavel

PREFACE

Welcome to Unpacking Yourself, a heartfelt gift of reflection and introspection crafted through poetry to illuminate the journey of self-discovery and personal growth. As my debut collection, this book is more than just a compilation of verses; it is a tender offering meant to guide you in rediscovering the little star within us all.

In the pages that follow, you will encounter a series of evocative poems designed to light the path to embracing your true self. Each poem is a reflection and an invitation, crafted to help you explore the depths of your inner world and reconnect with the brilliance that resides within. The lyrical prose and contemplative insights are intended to be both a companion and a mirror, reflecting the unique journey you undertake in your quest for self-understanding.

The inspiration behind 'Unpacking Yourself' springs from a profound belief that within each person lies a hidden light, a spark waiting to be discovered or rediscovered. As you turn each page, may you find solace, inspiration, and a renewed sense of connection with your own inner star. This book is a gift to you—a means to navigate the complexities of your heart and mind, and to embrace the essence of who you truly are.

Thank you for joining me on this voyage. I hope that these poems serve as a guiding light, enriching your path and offering encouragement as you explore and embrace your own journey of self-discovery.

May this book be a source of illumination and encouragement as you uncover the little star that shines within you.

With warm regards,
Dhamini Kandhavel

Gifted to Yourself!

Gifted to Yourself!
-From Yourself!

"Once upon a time..."
A classic way
to start a story.
"Twinkle Twinkle Little Star!"
A poem that
always comes to mind.
Once upon a time,
you were
the little superstar
in your own eyes!

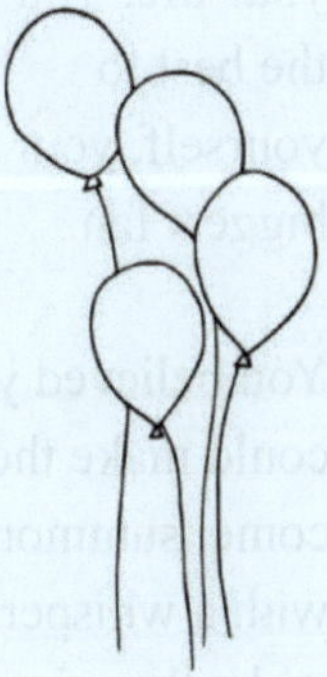

Remember the times
when you watched
your favorite action movie,
the thrilling scenes
setting your heart
ablaze, favorite romantic film,
dreaming of love's
sweet embrace, favorite cartoon,
where every frame
sparked laughter and joy,
a famous superhero flick,

where you donned
the cape in
your mind, or
a beloved princess tale,
where you danced
in castles of light?

You saw yourself
in the lead...
imagining you were
the hero of
your life. You were
the best to
yourself, your own
biggest fan.

You believed you
could make the rain
come, summon it
with a whispered wish,
make the rain
go, banish it
with a mere glance,
make people love
you, with just
a smile so bright,
and move the leaf
with a mere thought,
commanding nature's might.

You felt the power
within, the power
to control, the power
of self-love, the power
over everything, over
each and everything!

With a heart
full of dreams, you
saw magic in
everyday moments. You believed
in your own
extraordinary abilities, no
challenge too great,
no dream too big.
Your imagination soared, painting
the world with
vibrant hues of
possibility.

Sometimes, your power
didn't work on
everything. Sometimes, someone
or something shook
your belief, left
you questioning your magic,
questioning your little star.

When your small tricks
didn't work as expected,
when you couldn't
throw webs from
your hands, when
you realized you
weren't the red
Power Ranger, when
you saw you
weren't the lover
of your favorite actor,
when you discovered
you didn't have
those angel wings,
didn't possess that
Superman cape, didn't
wear that Cinderella gown,
didn't own that
super crayon box
to color your dreams.

When you couldn't
chase away the ghost
under your bed or
in your cupboard,
when you were bullied
at school but
couldn't stand against them.

When you were
no longer the
adorable kid in
your family and
missed being that,
when you weren't
the favorite person
of your favorite person
and wanted to
be always, when
your cuteness wasn't
cute anymore but
you tried your
best to be.

When you realized
you couldn't always
be the hero
to your parents
but tried your
best to prove
them wrong. When
you found you
were expected to
be a super
duper hero even
when you were
the superhero. When
you were judged

by your marks,
not by your talent,
when you were
placed in the
wrong school or
college, but the
only choice was
to go through.

When you were
disliked by someone
for no reason
but still wondered
about the reason.
When you wanted
to be like
someone else and
didn't understand the
comparison. When you
didn't get your
dream job and
accepted whatever job
you got. When
everyone else was
building forts, you
were still trying
to move a brick.

When everyone reached
their destination, and
you were still
wondering what's yours.
When everyone finished
their marathon, and
you didn't know
why you were
running at all.
When everyone's world
was colorful, and
your world was
blank everywhere. When
everyone had the
dictionary of their
life, but you
were still searching
for the meaning
of life.

Sometimes, you weren't
able to face
anything, you weren't
able to handle
things, you weren't
able to decide
anything. You may
have lived just
for the sake

of someone else—
or because you
weren't brave enough
to die.

But do you
know? You were
the bravest one,
and you still
are. You gathered
all the shattered
pieces of yourself,
and you made
that little superstar
in you shine
still. All you
need to understand
is, just realize
that little star
is still inside
you, always twinkling
within you. Don't
wonder, just realize
who you are.

And your world
is in your
hands and not
so high! You
are like that
diamond in the
sky!

Deep down, your
inner self knew
you were still
that superstar, shining
bright and true.
Embrace the magic
within, let your
dreams take flight.
You are unique,
precious, and endlessly
capable.

Remember, always, that
you are the
hero of your
own story, that
you are and
always will be
your own little
superstar, whose light
guides your way.

A reminder that
any gift is
special, not just
for what it
is, but for
who gives it.
And these words,
a gift, from
yourself, from your
own little superstar,
to yourself, a
reminder that you
are still that
superstar, a treasure
of self-love and
inspiration, waiting to
be rediscovered!

Unwrapping the present!

As a little kid,
gift in hand,
Eyes wide open,
thoughts expand.

What's inside?
Such joy to see,
Wrapped so bright,
what could it be?

A sparkle shines,
from tiny eyes,
Heartbeats quicken,
in surprise.

Colorful paper,
tied with bow,
Little hands,
unwrap it slow.

All excitement,
in that wrap,
What's inside,
a secret trap.

Without the wrap,
plain to know,
No thrill there,
no eyes aglow.

Like a pearl,
in its shell,
Like secrets,
oceans tell.

Like a bud,
yet to bloom,
Like stars hidden,
by the moon.

Like a moon,
in the day,
Like night,
masking gray.

Like a book,
closed so tight,
Like a dawn,
before light.

Like a chest,
locked away,
Like night sky,
masking day.

Like a seed,
in the earth,
Like a wish,
seeking birth.

Like a song,
unsung, sweet,
Like a mask,
fooling street.

Like a flame,
hid in night,
Like truth,
veiled in light.

Masked with smiles,
hiding pain,
Masked with courage,
facing rain.

Masked with norms,
righteous held,
Masked with lies,
truth expelled.

Masked with "ok,"
when we're not,
Masked with peace,
battles fought.

Masked with cheer,
grief concealed,
Masked with strength,
fears revealed.

Masked with pride,
humble heart,
Masked with calm,
falling apart.

Masked with joy,
tears inside,
Masked with words,
truths we hide.

There's a tale,
in every you,
Wrapped tight,
in secret view.

We have layers,
on us all,
Knowingly wrapped,
or in thrall.

A beautiful you,
layers deep,
Unwrap yourself,
no secrets keep.

People judge,
as they do,
But remember,
you are true.

Come out,
shed the layers made,
Show your light,
never fade.

Some keep wrappers,
safe and bright,
Some tear down,
with all their might.

Some will crush,
some discard,
But the wrap's,
just a guard.

A shield to hide,
a shield to show,
It's just a wrap,
not who we know.

The real gift,
is you inside,
Strip the layers,
do not hide.

We know deep,
inside us,
How we are,
who we are now.

It's not what,
you truly are,
It's what you,
show so far.

Pulled into,
life's demands,
Changed by life's,
unseen hands.

Once an extrovert,
now withdrawn,
Or introvert,
now acting strong.

Wishes wrapped,
by commitments tight,
Dreams for family,
hide from sight.

Ambitions shelved,
for others' sake,
Hopes in shadows,
choices fake.

Talents buried,
by daily grind,
Passions left,
far behind.

Remember one thing,
you are wrapped,
By yourself,
or perhaps trapped.

Time to unwrap,
like the sun,
Free the day,
when night is done.

Time for candles,
to pierce the night,
Time for butterflies,
to take flight.

Like the river,
unwraps from ice,
Like true love,
unwraps from lies.

Like the wind,
unwraps the leaves,
Like warm spring,
unwraps the freeze.

And finally,
it's the time,
When you unwrap,
yourself in rhyme.

Hey little star,
unwrap your light,
From the darkness,
shine so bright.

Twinkle now,
for all to see,
The real you,
set free to be!

Embracing the emotions!

As a kid,
or grown-up,
You know someone
brought a gift,
Holding it
in their hand,
To give you
a moment's lift.

You know it's
meant for you,
Can't wait to
see it through,
But you mask
your eager face,
Pretending not
to pursue.

Sometimes you wait
to open,
Till the guests
have all gone,
Other times you
can't wait,
And the wrapping
quickly drawn.

Excitement builds
with each unwrapping,
Curiosity takes flight,
Joy in the
surprise it brings,
Yet the gift
remains out of sight.

A little kid
stands there,
With all emotions
bare,
Reflecting how
you are now,
With feelings laid
so bare.

Excitement for
little things,
Joy in what
love brings,
Feeling cherished,
just as you
are, grateful for
gifts afar.

Satisfaction in
tasks complete,
Sadness when
no one understands,
Disappointment when
plans don't meet,
Worries held
in hand.

Stressed from
proving worth,
Tired from
pleasing others,
Anxiety climbing
high, fear
of stumbling, covers.

Loneliness shadows
close, anger
ignites a flare,
Hope lights up
the darkest nights,
Peace finds its
way there.

Confusion when
paths diverge,
Frustration with
unmet goals,

Yearning for
something more,
Contentment's still
unknown.

In one long
night, when
your room's doors
are shut tight,
Wrapped in
the bedsheet's fold,
Emotions unfold
in the night.

On a random
day, a
sudden bath
to clear the
fray, wishing
to wash away
the emotions
that sway.

Most of yourself,
most of the
time, escapes
the feelings behind
a phone's
bright chime.

At work, you
feign calm, hiding
the inner storm,
When you're shattered
inside, trying
to stay warm.

In crowded spaces,
you mask
your silent cries,
Hiding the tears
with a practiced
guise.

Each little kid
handles emotions
in their own
way, or side-steps
them as
feelings sway.

But instead
of running, face
the tides within,
Embrace your emotions,
let the healing
begin.

Explore each feeling,
from joy
to despair,
In every wave
of emotion, find
strength beyond
compare.

Handling emotions,
like a little kid,
Unwrapping life
with wonder amid.

Embracing each wave,
from laughter
to tears,
Every high
and low, through
joys and fears.
Like a child
with a gift,
You face
what’s to come,
With your heart
wide open,
to all
that is done.

Every twist
and turn,
Every ebb
and flow,
You meet
each emotion,
with courage
to grow.
Unwrapping the layers,
with a heart
sincere,
You cherish
each feeling,
both distant
and near.

For in each
emotion, there's
a lesson
to find,
A chance
to grow stronger,
With a heart
aligned.
Like a little
star that
twinkles bright,

You embrace
every feeling,
with all
of your might.

That little star,
handles it all,
Twinkling bright,
standing tall,
Embracing every
emotion's wave,
Still twinkling,
ever brave!

Unboxing the Present!

A little kid,
Unboxing the gift..!

A heart full of dreams,
Hands trembling with glee,
What will it be?
The excitement runs free.

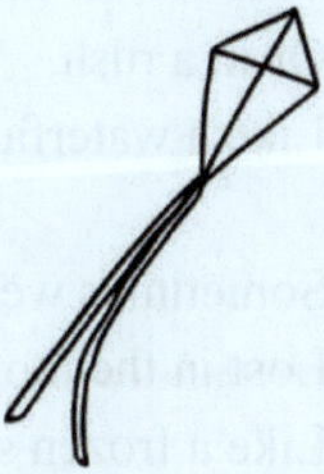

Will it be a car,
Racing to and fro?
Or a Barbie doll,
In her world of dreams?

The paper comes off,
In a flurry, a rush,
Tiny fingers fumble,
With an eager hush.

His eyes shine bright,
Like stars in the night,
Each tear of the wrap,
Brings more delight.

He can’t wait to see,
What magic it hides,
The thrill of the moment,
Is a joyous ride.

Sometimes with care,
We touch the box,
Like a delicate flower,
Fragile on the stalk.

Other times slow,
Like clouds drifting by,
Or in a rush,
Like a waterfall's cry.

Sometimes we pause,
Lost in the moment,
Like a frozen stream,
In the winter's lament.

But soon enough,
We'll find the truth,
Life's hidden gift,
Unveiled at last.

We watch others soar,
Running their own race,
At a different pace,
To reach their place.

While we feel stuck,
In life's winding maze,
Wondering when,
We'll see brighter days.

Some move like a breeze,
Swift and free,
While others take time,
Like a growing tree.

Some rise with the dawn,
In a burst of light,
Others find their spark,
In the quiet of the night.

Everyone runs,
At their own speed,
Everyone achieves,
As destined, indeed.

So enjoy the path,
Though the end's unclear,
For the journey itself,
Is a treasure, little star.

The path unfolds gently,
With each step you take,
Through valleys and peaks,
For your dreams' sake.

Every moment of waiting,
Every twist and turn,
Shapes the story you're writing,
In the fire you burn.

In the stillness of twilight,
Or the rush of the dawn,
Your spirit's unyielding,
And your courage reborn.

Like a story unfolding,
Page by wondrous page,
The script of your journey,
Is penned by your sage.

The laughter and tears,
The joy and the strife,
Each experience adds,
To the richness of life.

The world spins in colors,
In hues dark and light,
Each shade is a part
Of your dazzling flight.

When shadows loom large,
And doubts cloud your view,
Remember your essence,
And the light that is you.

The stars in their splendor,
The moon's gentle grace,
Mirror the beauty
In your radiant face.

With each passing moment,
As you grow and you learn,
The world becomes richer,
With each twist and turn.

So keep your heart open,
To the wonders you find,
For the magic is woven,
In the threads of your mind.

Every day's a new gift,
Wrapped in mystery's veil,
Unbox it with wonder,
And let your dreams sail.

Even if roads are rugged,
And paths seem unclear,
Your spirit will guide you,
Through each hope and fear.

Every challenge you meet,
Is a step in the dance,
A rhythm, a heartbeat,
In the song of chance.

As seasons keep changing,
And time flows like streams,
Hold fast to your dreams,
And the light that redeems.

So cherish the journey,
With its highs and its lows,
For the journey itself,
Is where true magic grows.

Hey little star,
If you run or you walk,
If you dance or you crawl,
If you fly or you swim,
Unless you stand still or shy from the try,
You'll twinkle in time,
Brighter than now,
Brighter than you can ever know !!!

Waiting for the Present!

Into a world
Buried deep inside you,

A little kid
Awoke in morning's light,
Nestled in bed,
Wrapped tight with love,
Earth's scent kissing the nose,
Rain's whisper in the ear,
Eyes half-open,
Glimpsing through window screens,
A drizzle's gentle dance,
The little kid's heart
Hoping, praying,
For a rainy day's delight,
An unexpected holiday.

A little kid
Scribbles furiously,
Lost in ink and paper,
Dreams flowing in every line,
Eager to finish,
Hoping for a sweet respite,
Yearning for a break,
From endless exams,

The joy of holidays
Hangs in the balance.

A little kid
Carefree, untouched by pain,
Sweat gleaming like dew,
Dirt-smeared,
Racing home,
Heaven’s aroma calling,
Mom’s favorite dish on the stove,
The little kid’s heart leaps,
Anticipating the taste,
Of home-cooked warmth.

A little kid
In awe of simple joys,
Eyes wide with wonder,
Waiting for every small delight,
Rainbows after storms,
Stars in the night,
The thrill of new toys,
Whispers of bedtime stories,
Summer’s endless days,
Winter’s first snowfall,
Moments cherished and held,
With innocent wonder.

Just like that little kid,
We often wait,
Sometimes too impatiently,
For dreams to unfurl,
In every hidden corner,
In the quiet spaces,
We yearn for miracles,
For the mundane to sparkle,
For life to unfold in grace,
In both grand and small ways.

We wait for peace,
To hold our loved ones close,
To solve financial woes,
To journey to favorite places,
To taste simple joys,
To find solace in everyday moments,
To embrace what life gives.

The little star within,
Yearns for miracles,
For dreams to take flight,
For small things to shine,
In the present's embrace,
Don't forget the now,
The essence of you,
In every waiting moment,
What's meant for you
Will always find its way.

In patience, we find worth,
In waiting, we find grace,
For the little star within,
To twinkle like a supernova,
Shining bright after waiting,
Radiant and whole.

Hey little star,
While waiting for
The future to unfold,
Don't forget the present,
The now in your heart,
The moments that start.

Embrace each minute,
As it quietly sings,
For waiting too long
Can snatch joy's small things.

In every heartbeat,
In each breath you take,
Find beauty in now,
For its own sake.

In the midst of patience,
In the silent prayers,
Find strength to persevere,
Through life's fleeting layers.

As each day dawns anew,
Let hope gently rise,
For in every sunrise,
A new opportunity lies.

Don't rush through moments,
Let them unfold with grace,
In the waiting, there's wisdom,
In the now, a sacred space.

In the quiet of dawn,
In the whispers of dusk,
Find the rhythm of waiting,
In dreams and in trust.

Cherish each small wonder,
In the grand dance of time,
For every fleeting second
Is a moment so sublime.

Hey little star,
When dreams seem far away,
Remember, in the waiting,
Joy finds its way.

In every heartbeat,
In every breath's embrace,
The essence of life
Is found in its pace.

Embrace the journey,
With patience and cheer,
For every star shines brightest
When its time draws near.

Hey little star,
It’s all worth the wait,
Every moment of patience,
For the star that glows,
In the heart of you,
Waiting to twinkle bright!!!

The Manufacturing Defect !

An empty land once
Filled with nature's grace.
A few drops fall,
To become an ocean.
Water flows freely,
Creating beautiful falls.
Leaves gently fall,
Bringing autumn's charm.

Carbon pressed hard,
Turns into diamond.
Flowing gold becomes
Astonishing ornaments crafted.
Simple shell hides
A precious pearl.

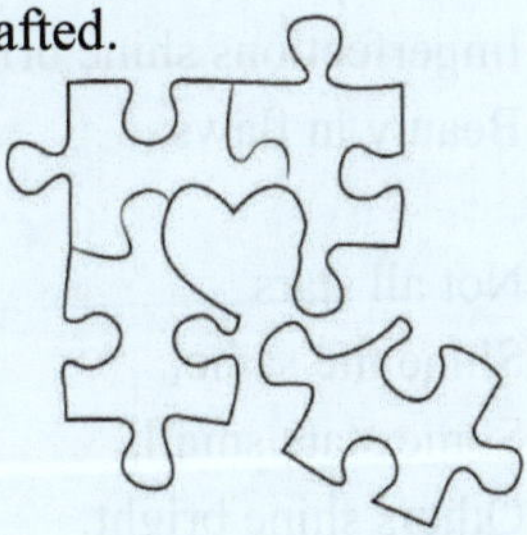

Caterpillar crawls slow,
Becomes a butterfly.
Dark clouds loom,
Day turns bright.
A seed sprouts,
Becomes a tree.
Echo fades away,
Voice remains strong.

How the sky
In favorite colors?
How the water
If it's colorful?

Dream of skies
Hues we adore.
Imagine seas,
Colors galore.

Each thing made
With purpose clear.
Imperfections hold beauty,
Flaws unique charm.
Crafted with care,
Yet not perfect.
Imperfections shine bright,
Beauty in flaws.

Not all stars
Shine the same.
Some stars small,
Others shine bright.
Each star glows,
In its way.
Hidden lights gleam,
Bearing no shame.

Hey little star,
Shine in you.
Adore yourself deeply,
Flaws and all.
Keep on twinkling,
Better each day.

Flaws are gifts,
Lessons in disguise.
Growth through failure,
Myth of perfection.
Beauty lies within,
Embrace your journey.
Life begins now.

Not all perfect,
Sometimes imperfect too.
Imperfections make beautiful,
In unique ways.
Manufactured uniquely,
Different and true.
Sometimes defective,
Making you effective.

Stars all different,
Visible or not.
Shine your light,
Big or small.
Twinkle your way,
Bright and brighter.

Be the star
You are meant to.
Twinkle high,
Wild and free.
Adore your light,
Inside you shines.
Shine every day,
Far and wide.

Hey little star,
Glimmer so true.
Universe is yours,
Belongs to you.
Through each night,
And every day.
Keep on twinkling,
In your way!

Nature's design, unique,
No two are the same.
Mountains high, low,
Valleys deep, wide.
Rivers winding paths,
Lakes serene calm.
Sunsets paint skies,
Dawns bring light.

Every flower blooms,
In its own time.
No rush needed,
Patience is key.
Beauty in waiting,
Growth in stillness.
Roots grow deep,
Strength unseen.

Imperfections teach us,
Lessons profound, clear.
Every scar tells,
A story untold.
Wear them proudly,
Badges of honor.
Life's journey shaped,
By trials faced.

Not all paths,
Straight and narrow.
Winding roads lead,
To destinations unknown.
Embrace the detours,
For they guide,
To places hidden,
Treasures inside.

Raindrops on leaves,
Tears of joy.
Storms pass by,
Rainbows appear.
Clear skies after,
Dark nights fade.
Hope always shines,
Through the gloom.

Imperfections and all,
You are enough.
Unique in form,
Perfectly you.
Keep shining bright,
In your own light.
Twinkle on,
Little star true.

Embrace your journey,
With open heart.
Trust in process,
Life's unfolding art.
Step by step,
Day by day.
Grow and learn,
Find your way.

Rain's soft patter,
On window pane.
Washes away,
Sorrow and pain.
Brings new life,
To earth below.
Seeds will sprout,
Begin to grow.

Snowflakes fall,
Unique and bright.
Blanket the earth,
In pure white.
Each one different,
Perfectly made.
Nature's wonder,
In snow displayed.

Every journey,
Step by step.
Paths we take,
None we regret.
Lessons learned,
Along the way.
Growth in heart,
Day by day.

Never forget.
Universe vast,
No regret.
Shine your light,
Bright and true.
Universe's gift,
Special you.

Hey little star,
Glimmer so true.
Universe is yours,
Belongs to you.
Through each night,
And every day.
For each day,
For each and everyday,
Keep on twinkling,
Better and better,
In your own way!
In your very own way!

The Mystery Gift!

A baby is born,
Tiny hands wave gently,
Soft cries fill air,
One day smiles appear.

That smile, a secret,
Bright as dawn's first light,
A mystery unfolds,
In its purest form.

How does it come?
From where does it spring?
A silent revelation,
A joy so profound.

A glimpse of wonder,
In the baby's gaze,
A gift of pure grace,
Wrapped in innocence's light.

Mystery softly whispers,
In every little grin,
A question left unanswered,
Yet filled with love within.

Mountains stand tall, firm,
Water flows freely, endless,
Stars twinkle so bright,
Universe expands beyond sight.

The ocean's depth, unknown,
Waves dance with the moon,
Forests whisper secrets,
Leaves rustle ancient tales.

Thunder rolls in silence,
Lightning paints the sky,
Volcanoes breathe fire,
Rivers carve their way.
all the way,

The universe remains a mystery,
In all ways!
Mysteries surround us always,
Humans are mysteries too,
leave unknown forever,
Some seek hidden truths.

Mysteries stay always unknown,
Things fall into place,
Beyond our grasp, reach,
Past our limited knowledge.

Hey, little star shining,
You hold a light,
Mystery within you glowing,
Shining so very bright.

Not a mystery, truly,
You will always shine,
Better, brighter each day,
No matter what comes.

Look inside, seek truth,
Life's a journey unfolding,
Find your way, path,
Embrace the mystery within.

Step by step, grow,
Learn, explore each day,
Each moment brings light,
Unfolding truths inside you.

You are a star,
In this vast sky,
Shine your light brightly,
Let it always guide.

Remember, always stay bright,
You are pure light,
In this endless night,
Shine, evolve, forever anew.

Life's a grand mystery,
You are a star,
Shining, evolving endlessly,
Forever beautifully new.

Mountains and rivers,
Skies and oceans deep,
Mysteries we ponder,
Secrets we keep.

The world holds secrets,
Ancient and profound,
Yet the human spirit,
Is equally renowned.

Nature's vast mysteries,
Echo our inner quest,
The unknown in the world,
Mirrors what's in our heart.

The cosmos' grand design,
Matches our inner maze,
Both hold vast mysteries,
Both set hearts ablaze.

From galaxies afar,
To the heart's hidden door,
Both worlds intertwine,
Mysteries to explore.

In every leaf and star,
In every dream and thought,
The world and our being,
Are mysteries sought.

So embrace the unknown,
Let curiosity guide,
In the dance of life,
Let your spirit glide.

In the quiet of night,
In the burst of the day,
Nature's secrets reveal,
In their own special way.

Life is a grand mystery,
A gift we hold dear,
Every moment is a chance,
To find what is near.

Hey, little star,
Whatever it may be,
It may be a mystery
That you have a little star in you,
But it's never a mystery
That the little star is twinkling
And will twinkle better and brighter,
No matter what!

Milestones as Gifts !

The little kid
In you, with
Tiny eyes, glazed
At a toy
In the distance,
Trying to crawl,
Fighting with the
Floor, and grabbing
The baby rattle
With small hands.

Seeing the toy
Below the stairs,
The little kid
In you
Not knowing
How to walk or
Even to take
The first step,
But saw
Not all the
Steps, but just
One step, wondering
How to climb,
Sitting on that

First step, to
Reach the next,
And finally, unknowingly,
Climbing all the
Way to the
Final step to
Claim the toy!

Excited for the
New cycle, wrapped
In covers still,
To ride it,
Though unsure how
To begin—legs pedaled,
Hands danced with
The handlebars! Like
A pilot, feeling
Like a racer,
Started to ride,
Happily to kiss
The road, falling
Heavily, like a
Shooting star, wounded
For life! To
Learn the first
Ride and ride
Forever!

When your name
Was called for
The first time,
Loud before all,
To step up
On stage, walking
Each step with
Fear, trying to
Hide shaking legs,
Gathered all the
Courage, yet stammered
Before everyone, landing
Trained to walk
Boldly, to at
Least have the
Courage to open
Up yourself in
Later days!

Day and night,
Worked very hard,
Eyes like islands
Surrounded by dark
Circles, learning anew,
Thinking you're low,
Thrived to be

Better, each day
Enhancing you, to
Earn hard bucks,
Only to vanish
With little mistakes!
Starting from the
Beginning, to pay
Back all the
Tears, sweat, and
Blood!

Through every fall
And stumble, you've
Learned to rise,
Finding strength in
Struggle, reaching for
The skies, in
Each challenge faced,
You've found your
Grace, with every
Setback, you've picked
Up the pace.

From crawling to
Soaring, from trembling
To be sure, you've
Embraced the journey,
With a heart
Pure, each milestone

Conquered, a testament
To your fight,
Shining ever brighter,
In the dark
Of the night.

The first step's
Wobbly path, a
Crawl that's full
Of might, the
Way you stretched
Your fingers, to
Grasp that toy
So tight. Moments
Of frustration, when
Nothing seemed to
Work, yet through
All the trials,
Your spirit never
Shirked.

The balance of
A bicycle, the
Thrill of every
Ride, through every
Fall and scrape,
You learned to
Enjoy the ride.
Each attempt a

Lesson, each scar
A mark of
Pride, turning pain
Into triumph, as
You faced the
World wide.

When the stage
Lights blazed, your
Heart raced with
Fear, yet with
Every trembling step,
You conquered the
Atmosphere. Your voice
Might have faltered,
But courage grew
Anew, with every
Hesitant word, a
Bold soul shone
Through.

In the grind
Of every day,
With shadows 'round
Your eyes, you
Toiled through sleepless
Nights, underneath the
Vast skies. Each
Mistake a teacher,

Each challenge a
Guide, turning your
Frustrations into fuel
For the ride.

You climbed each
Rung of progress,
With each milestone,
You grew, facing
Doubts and struggles,
Yet your vision
Stayed true. Building
Dreams from fragments,
With hands that
Shaped the clay,
Turning every hardship
Into light along
Your way.

From the first
Rattle's jingle, to
The echo of
A cheer, every
Moment built upon
The path you
Hold dear. The
Cycle's ups and
Downs, the stage's
Trembling light, each

Step forward teaches
You to reach
New heights.

In the quiet
Of the evening,
When the world
Seems so still,
Reflect on every
Challenge and the
Strength that you
Instill. Through the
Ups and downs
Of life, each
Test and every
Scar, you've forged
Your own path
Forward, shining like
A star.

Every stumble, every
Fall, every rise,
Every gain, each
Milestone that you
Conquer, turns into
Wisdom's refrain. Embracing
Every struggle, with
A heart that's

Brave and true,
You turn each
Moment into a
Testament to you.

The cycles that
You've ridden, the
Stages that you've
Faced, the dreams
You've chased so
Bravely, in every
Moment placed. All
These trials and
Triumphs, are milestones
In your story,
Each chapter of
Your journey, a
Testament to glory.

The echoes of
Your laughter, the
Whispers of your
Tears, they form
The melody of
All your growing
Years. Through each
Crescendo, each diminuendo,

You've learned to
Play your part,
With every note
And lyric, you've
Crafted from the
Heart.

So here's to
Every milestone, every
Step along the
Way, to the
Trials that have
Shaped you, and
The lessons they
Convey. With courage
As your compass,
And dreams that
Brightly burn, each
Moment, each achievement,
Is a victory
You've earned.

Life goes on,
Between the falls
And rises, balancing
Ups and downs,
Taking steps, crossing
Milestones, one by
One, learning, upgrading,

Improving with each
Fall—falling to rise,
Rising to shine.

Hey, little star!
Like a shooting
Star, for which
Falls everyone may
Await, but the
Star twinkles better
After each fall,
Better after every
Rise, better after
Every milestone!

The Timely Gift!

We measure time
In seconds,
Minutes,
Hours,
Days,
Years, and so on...

Time is a river,
Ever flowing, never stopping,
Sometimes slow, sometimes fast,
Shaping our lives,
From the past to the present,
And into the future unknown!

Sometimes,
Minutes stretch into hours,
Days flash by in a second,
Moments slipping through our fingers
Like grains of sand,
Each one unique,
Each one precious!

Time isn't always
Scientific;
It can weave a spell
For someone,
Creating memories
That linger forever
In the heart's deep recesses.

Some moments
Deserve to be frozen,
Captured like a photograph,
Etched into our minds,
Like a bright morning,
Lying on a bed of clouds
Beside your loved ones,
Watching them sleep
Like a kid,
Or your own kid even,
Peaceful and serene,
In the early dawn light.

Some moments
Deserve to be extended,
Stretched like a golden thread,
Like a vacation,
Amidst joy,
Savoring the breeze,
Exploring the world,
And discovering yourself,

Feeling the sun on your face,
The wind in your hair,
The freedom of being
In the moment,
Fully alive!

Some moments
Deserve to be forgotten,
Buried deep
Within your heart,
Never to be unearthed,
Like old wounds,
That have healed over time,
But still ache
In the quiet of the night,
Memories best left
In the shadows,
Unspoken,
Unseen.

Some moments
Deserve to be shortened,
When you find yourself
In discomfort,
In situations that make you uneasy,
Or to lessen the tedium
Of a long journey,
Wishing for time to fly,
For the hours to pass

Swiftly,
Like a bird in flight,
Carrying you to a place
Of comfort,
Of peace!

Some moments
Deserve to be cherished,
Held close to the heart,
Like happy days,
Holidays,
Time with family
And friends,
Laughter shared,
Tears wiped away,
The warmth of togetherness,
The bonds of love,
That time cannot break,
Memories that glow
With a golden light,
In the twilight of life!

Some moments
Deserve a second chance,
A chance to relive,
To feel again
The joy, the love,
The innocence of childhood,
Or the best times

With loved ones,
Or the instant
You first loved yourself,
Seeing yourself
Through kind eyes,
With a heart full of grace,
Knowing that you are
Enough,
Just as you are!

Every moment
Becomes a memory,
A thread in the tapestry
Of our lives,
But not every memory
Is cherished,
Some fade away,
Like whispers in the wind,
Others linger,
Like the scent of a rose,
Sweet and tender,
Reminding us
Of times gone by!

Nothing is permanent,
Nor is time.
As it's often said,
Time will pass,
Every moment will pass,

And you are
The constant,
The anchor in the storm,
The light in the dark,
The heart that beats
Steadily,
Through the changes,
Through the years!

So take each moment,
Hold it close,
Feel its pulse,
Its rhythm,
Let it dance
In your heart,
Like a song,
Like a prayer,
A whisper of grace,
In the silence of time.

For time is fleeting,
But the memories we create,
The love we share,
The dreams we chase,
These are eternal,
Written in the stars,
In the fabric of our souls!

So live,
Love,
Dream,
And be,
For time is a gift,
And you,
You are the miracle
In its flow,
The light in its passage,
The star that shines,
Bright and eternal,
In the endless night!

Hey, little star!
Time falls,
Time flows,
Time lingers,
Time races,
But the little star
In you
Remains,
In the present,
The past,
The future,
Even across dimensions,
The little star
In you was twinkling,
Now twinkles brighter,
And will twinkle
Eternally!!!

The Joy of Giving !

In smiles shared bright,
In hands held tight,
In moments warm,
In kindness' charm,
In hearts that touch…

Giving's river flows,
Soul to soul it goes,
A gentle stream,
Or a mighty beam,
Nurturing life's thread,
From the now to ahead.

A simple smile's grace,
Lights up any place!
Small acts ripple wide,
Golden grains beside,
Moments of pure cheer,
Beacons shining clear!

Like a mother's love,
Endless, pure above,
Her whole life's guide,
In giving, she abides.

A child's heartfelt hi,
A dog's love nearby,
A stranger's downcast plea,
Brightens with empathy!

In an orphanage day,
Excitement lights the way,
New faces more dear,
Than food's fleeting cheer.

In a world so vast,
Gifts of love will last!
A hug's warm embrace,
Turns dark to a grace,
A thoughtful deed,
Meets every soul's need.

A kind word can heal,
Wounds it will seal,
A laugh shared true,
Makes the heart renew!
In moments like these,
Joy flows with ease.

Gifts are not just things,
But the warmth they bring!
In actions so sweet,
Life's trials retreat,
Each gesture a song,
To which we belong!

In the quiet of night,
When the sky is dark,
Stars shine so bright!
Ignite a spark!
Each twinkle a guide,
Guiding with their glow,
Their warmth we bestow,
To those lost and cold,
Hearts turn to gold.

A warm cup of tea,
Shared joyfully,
Brews comfort anew,
In every sip true!
In cold winter's grip,
Love's warmth does slip.

As the bonfire's soft glow,
Warms the night's slow,
A shared moment's worth,
Brings light to the earth!
In cozy companionship,
Life's burdens will slip.

In the park's gentle breeze,
A child's laugh brings ease!
In nature's simple grace,
Peace finds its place,
In every game played,
A love that won't fade.

A book's open page,
Turns life's stage!
With each story told,
Hearts are consoled,
In the magic of lore,
Love opens the door.

In a rainy day's charm,
The shared umbrellas
Keep warm!
In shared raindrops' dance,
Hearts find their chance,
To offer their cover,
To help one another.

A kind word spoken true,
Like the morning dew,
Freshens the spirit,
With a soft, warm merit!
In moments of grace,
Kindness finds its place.

When the dawn breaks clear,
With the sun's first cheer,
A morning's warm light,
Turns darkness to bright!
In every sunrise gift,
Life's spirits uplift!

A gentle hand's touch,
Means so very much!
In a moment's embrace,
Finds a sacred place,
In every shared glance,
Love's deep romance.

A soft song's refrain,
Lifts hearts from pain!
In melodies sweet,
Finds a rhythm to beat,
In music's pure art,
Healing starts.

As the sun dips low,
In twilight's warm glow,
A shared evening's peace,
Brings love's release!
In moments still,
Hearts find their will.

Sometimes giving means,
A sacrifice unseen,
A part of ourselves,
Freely given, it delves,
Into our own soul,
To make another whole.

True joy in giving,
Is from the heart's living!
Not for pride or show,
But for love's pure glow,
To give with delight,
Makes every gift right!

In your own special way,
Give with heart and soul,
And make others whole!
The time is now,
To lift hearts somehow,
For joy in giving true,
Begins with you!

Hey, little star bright,
Twinkle with your light!
Make others glow,
With your warmth bestow!
For in giving you'll find,
The joy that twinkles!!!

On the Way !

To the hill,
The car glides
Like a bird
In a smooth flight!

Windows adorned
With falling pearls,
A delicate scatter.

Every rise and fall,
Every turn,
Unfolds like a rainbow
On the ground,
Each hairpin bend
A vivid curve.

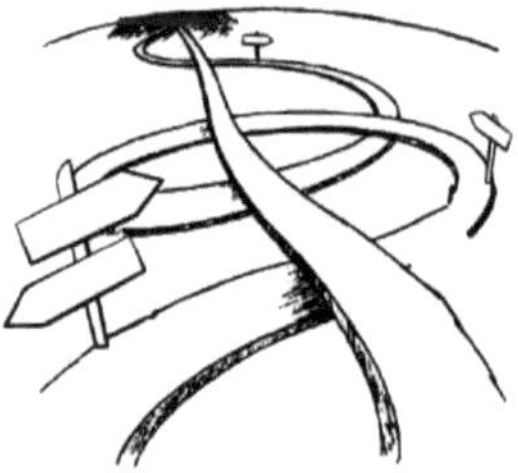

Sometimes you're pushed forward,
Sometimes pulled back,
Sometimes you sway left,
Sometimes right.

At the next turn,
You brace yourself.
At the next descent,
You grip tight.

It's all experience,
It's all learning
On the way.

On the way,
You might pause
For hot tea,
Or a cooling ice cream.
You might stop
For the view,
Or search for
Roasted, spicy corn.

On the way,
You might dream
Of settling
In a tranquil hilltop life.
But then you see
An old granny
With trembling hands,
Making Maggi,
Working hard to make ends meet,
Weary of nature,
Exhausted by life,
And you rethink
What life means.

Life goes on.
On the way,
You learn,
You realize,
You change,
You improve.

On the way,
Like the moon
That travels with you,
Glowing,
Smiling back,
Wondering why
It's by your side,
Shedding light
To guide you,
Like the
Little star within you,
With you
Throughout your journey.

Hey, little star!
You are
On the way,
Twinkling brighter
Each day.

On the way,
Moments pass,
Guiding light
Shining bright
In the night.

On the way,
With bold dreams,
Stories told,
In your glow
Hearts will know
Love's warm flow.

On the way,
On paths you tread,
Light is spread,
Hope you'll weave
As you leave
Gifts to believe.

On the way,
When shadows fall,
Stand tall,
In the dark
Be the spark
Make your mark.

On the way,
Through every storm,
Keep warm,
Shine through rain,
Easing pain,
Hope will reign.

On the way,
As dawn breaks clear,
Never fear,
In your light,
Day and night
Hearts take flight.

On the way,
In fields, you cross,
No loss,
In your shine,
Love will find
Peace divine.

On the way,
With every step,
Don't forget,
You inspire,
Hearts on fire,
To aspire.

On the way,
On nights so deep,
As we sleep,
Dreams take flight,
With your light,
All is right.

On the way,
With each new dawn,
Carry on,
In your gleam,
Live the dream,
Be the beam.

On the way,
When times are tough,
Be enough,
With your grace,
Fill the space,
Hearts embrace.

On the way,
In skies so wide,
Side by side,
Light the way,
Day by day,
Come what may.

On the way,
When least expected,
A partner appears,
Sharing joys,
Easing fears.

On the way,
With them beside,
Life's beauty blooms,
Love as our guide.

On the way,
Together we strive,
Making memories,
Feeling alive.

On the way,
In their embrace,
Life's meaning deepens,
A loving space.

Hey, little star!
You are
On the way,
Twinkling brighter
Every day.

So little star,
Near or far,
On your way,
Twinkle bright,
Every day!

Between expectations and reality !

On a fine evening,
A little star,
Returned from school,
Kicked off shoes,
Tossed the bag,
Unbuttoned the shirt,
Sat before the TV,
To enjoy a favorite show,
With a favorite dish.

Dwelled in the
Power of superheroes,
Imagined being
A superhero.
Expected to
Fly and fight,
But in reality,
Fell hard
To the ground.
Reality hits
Hard sometimes.

Expected to be
The hero,
But in reality,
Becoming
The beloved
Side actor.

Expected to be
In the dream job,
But in reality,
Landing
In some random job.

Expected to
Be brave like a king,
But in reality,
Forced to be a coward.

Expected to
Voice out,
But in reality,
Forced to shut up.

Expectation whispers,
Promises sweet,
Reality steps in,
With challenges to meet.

In a lush garden,
The little star saw blooms bright,
A paradise of flowers,
In morning's light.

Expectation planted
Seeds of pure delight,
But reality brought
Pests in the night.

The little star toiled and tended,
Through sun and rain,
Reality's harsh touch,
Yet growth's gain.

For in the thorns,
And weeds that grew,
The little star found beauty,
In resilience too.

A student's mind,
Filled with ambition's fire,
Expectations high,
To rise ever higher.

Books and grades,
A future clear,
But reality showed
Struggles near.

Late nights of study,
Tests that daunt,
Reality's trials,
And endless want.

Yet in each failure,
A lesson learned,
In every stumble,
Strength was earned.

For expectation dreams,
Of perfect scores,
Reality teaches,
To strive for more.

In love's sweet song,
The little star sought a tune,
Expectations high,
Beneath the moon.

Pictured romance,
Without flaw,
A seamless dance,
Without a pause.

But reality's rhythm,
Had its own beat,
With steps that faltered,
And hearts' heat.

Misunderstandings,
Moments of strife,
Yet through it all,
A deeper life.

For expectation paints,
A picture grand,
Reality shapes,
With its own hand.

In a career's climb,
The little star saw the peak,
Expectations high,
A journey unique.

Success seemed close,
Within sight,
But reality brought
Long days and nights.

Challenges rose,
Obstacles tall,
Reality's call,
Testing it all.

Yet in each trial,
The little star found a way,
With every setback,
A brighter day.

In friendship's bond,
The little star hoped for gold,
Expectations high,
Stories untold.

Pictured laughter,
Trust without end,
But reality's hand,
Did sometimes bend.

Miscommunications,
Distances grew,
Reality tested,
The bonds once knew.

Yet in the trials,
And times apart,
The little star found true friends,
With an open heart.

For expectation dreams,
Of perfect ties,
Reality shows,
Where true strength lies.

In every goal,
And every quest,
Expectations rise,
Reality tests.

Expectation's light,
Guides the way,
Reality's touch,
Shapes the day.

It might not
Be the expected
Gift, but gift
Is more beautiful
When received unexpectedly
Or beyond the
Expectations. In reality,
Every gift is
Beautiful in its
Own way.

Hey, little star!
For in the dance,
Between the two,
Between
The expectation and
The reality,
We find our path,
And twinkle through!!!

The Judgmental Gift

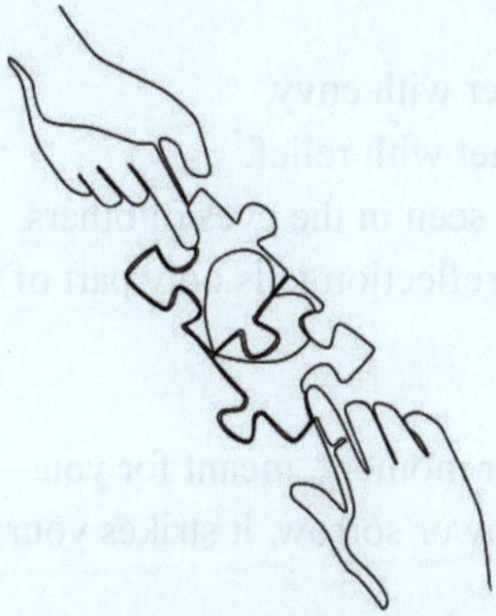

Sometimes our happiness is the reason for others' sadness,
And our joy, a silent weight on someone else's heart.
Surprisingly, our grief brings comfort to another,
As if our tears wash away their hidden scars.
What we cherish as a blessing
Might become a burden in someone else's world,
And our surprises turn into others' frustrations,
Like gifts unopened, left to gather dust.

The path we walk with pride
Might seem like a shadow to another,
And the light we seek to find
Can blind the eyes of those beside us.

How strange it is to witness
The mirrors of our lives reflect a distorted truth—
A smile met with envy,
A frown met with relief.
Yet what's seen in the eyes of others,
But every reflection tells only part of the truth!

It's all your moment, meant for you—
Whether joy or sorrow, it strikes your heart.

How much that wave threw you back.
All joy, earned through dark circles, sleepless nights, and many falls.
If it's failure, people will pity you.
If it's need, people will vanish.
If it's success, they'll say it's luck.
But only you know what you've endured.

Stick to the true ones, even if they're few.
It's better to walk alone than with the wrong crowd,
Just because you fear walking alone.

No gift is just a gift—it's a reward!
In the daylight, you can't see the stars,
But that doesn't mean they're not there.
They' re always twinkling, no matter what,
And people's words can't stop them from
shining,
Only you know the journey that fuels your glow!

Yes, twinkle, twinkle, little star—
Even if they wonder how you are!
Only you know how you're going up above,
And what makes you shine,
Like a diamond with strength and love!

The Gifted Map of Moods!

On this journey,
The map unfolds,
Guiding the path
Shaped by moods—

The mood,
Leading you north,
Only to have
A sudden swing
Throw you south!

One moment,
The mood directs you east,
Then, without warning,
Pulls you west!

Emotions balance,
Shifting,
Affected by
What lies within
And what surrounds you.

A bad mood day
Turns brighter
With just a few words
From loved ones—

Fed up with running,
A machine worn and weary,
Your mood shifts
In a heartbeat
By reflecting
On why you began to run!

Mood changes aren't always
Self-contained;
Sometimes they are shaped
By what's around.

After an exhaustive day,
Hours of toil and strain,
Every bone aching,
The mood darkens.
Yet, the sudden patter of rain,
Birdsong's gentle hum,
And the earth's fresh scent
Lift your spirits!

A happy day begins,
Hopeful to end
As it started,
Bright and joyous.
But in a moment,
A few careless words
From someone dear
Shatter the joy,
Fracturing your emotions.

So whenever
You say you're zoned out,
Or in a bad mood,
Or your mood suddenly shifts,
It doesn't just alter your day—
It also affects
Those around you!

The map of moods
Is never still;
It's constantly evolving,
A reflection of the heart.
Paths twist and turn,
Guided by the inner storms,
Whispered hopes,
And the gentle breezes
Of what is.

Every sunrise brings
A new shade to the map,
A fresh palette
Of potential moods.
What begins as calm
Can swiftly shift,
Colors blending
Into a canvas
Of ever-changing hues!

When the world feels heavy,

And your mood is low,
Remember,
The map is not fixed.
It bends and weaves
With each passing moment,
Offering new directions
And fresh starts.

In the quiet of twilight,
When shadows dance
And stars awaken,
The map's contours
Are illuminated
By the glow of distant lights,
Guiding you through
The darkest hours.

A sudden burst of laughter,
A kind word spoken,
Can shift the map's path,
Realigning your course
With warmth and light.
Such is the power
Of connection,
Of shared moments
That uplift the spirit.

As the moon waxes and wanes,
So do the moods,
Shifting with the phases
Of life’s ebb and flow.
The tides of emotion
Rise and fall,
Guided by the unseen forces
That shape our hearts.

But beware,
For the map is not always
Predictable or clear.
It is marked with uncertainties,
And sometimes,
You’ll find yourself
Lost in the maze
Of shifting moods.

Yet even in confusion,
There’s beauty.
The map’s intricate patterns,
The way they intertwine,
Speak of the complexity
Of our inner worlds.
They remind us that
Every shift, every change,
Is a part of the grand design.

A gentle breeze on a summer's day,
The warmth of the sun
On your face,
Can shift your mood
As swiftly as a storm.
Such is the nature of existence—
Ever-changing, ever-moving,
Guided by forces
Beyond our control.

In the quiet moments,
When all is still,
The map reveals
Its hidden paths.
It's here you can trace
The journey of your soul,
The winding roads
Of joy and sorrow,
Of triumph and defeat.

So when the days are long
And the nights are dark,
Look at the map
Of your moods,
And find solace
In its ever-changing patterns.
It's a reflection of you,
A testament to your journey,
A guide through the storms
And the calm.

As you navigate
The map of your moods,
Remember,
You are never alone.
Each shift, each change,
Is a part of the journey,
A part of the map
That makes up
The beautiful mosaic
Of your existence.

Embrace the fluctuations,
Celebrate the highs,
And learn from the lows.
The map will always
Guide you forward,
Through every twist and turn,
Until you find
Your true course,
Your true self.

Like a river
That alters its course
When it meets
The forces around it,
Shifting its path
With every influence.

Hey, little star,
You are the star
On this map,
A gift to the sky,
Balancing the moods of the heavens.
Just as the plain dark sky
Is beautified
By the twinkling stars,
So too are you,
A lighthouse in the map,
Twinkling the path for all!

The Return Policy!

The returns
In heartfelt apologies,
In second chances,
In words unsaid,
In deeds undone,
And in hopes rekindled...!

Returns are a journey,
A path back to grace,
Sometimes a winding road,
Sometimes a swift embrace,
Mending lives,
From the fragmented past,
To a harmonious future reborn.

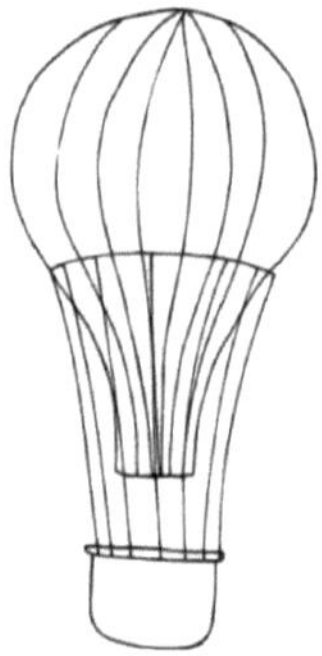

Sometimes,
An apology can mend a heart,
A second chance can blossom anew,
Moments of reconciliation slipping through our fingers
Like precious threads of trust,
Each one a renewal,
Each one a promise.

Some moments
Deserve to be reclaimed,
Captured like a second sunrise,
Etched into our minds,
Like a forgiven mistake,
A heartfelt embrace,
A tender smile,
Brightening the path forward,
In the quiet dawn light.

Some chances
Deserve to be granted,
Stretched like a golden thread,
Like a renewed friendship,
Amidst joy,
Bringing peace,
Exploring the depth of forgiveness,
And discovering the self,
Feeling the lightness in your step,
The calm in your heart,
The freedom of mending
In the moment,
Fully alive.

Some regrets
Deserve to be released,
Let go into the wind,
Like old burdens,
That have weighed on us over time,
Easing the ache
In the still of the night,
Memories best set free,
Spoken,
Released.

Some gestures
Deserve to be cherished,
Held close to the heart,
Like apologies made,
Wrongs righted,
The warmth of reconciliation,
The bonds of renewed trust,
That time cannot break,
Moments that glow
With a golden light,
In the twilight of life.

Some mistakes
Deserve a second chance,
A chance to right the wrongs,
To feel again
The joy, the love,
The relief of forgiveness,

Or the best times
When we made amends,
Or the instant
We first sought redemption,
Seeing ourselves
Through kind eyes,
With a heart full of grace,
Knowing that we are
Redeemed,
Just as we are.

It's always best to return back
Whatever we get,
Love as love,
Kindness as gratitude,
Hurt as a sorry,
Misunderstanding as clarity,
Anger with calm,
Dishonesty with truth,
Fear with courage,
Sadness with cheer,
Doubt with trust,
Neglect with care,
Conflict with peace,
And despair with hope!

Hey, little star!
You twinkle
Sometimes
When someone
Sacrifices their twinkle
For you!
That twinkle
You got
Needs to be returned
For someone to twinkle!
Twinkle and let twinkle!

The Shipment Delayed!

In the morning's light,
Birds sing their gentle
Tune, as you rush
To paint a canvas
With golden hue on
A brown bordered
White square.
But a touch too
Much, and it turned
Black. No choice but
To start anew, now
Creating a perfect
Bread Toast, just right.

Yet, the day's plans
Falter; arriving late, you
Discover you missed a
Train—one that encountered
Trouble. Your delay, though
Frustrating, shielded you
From harm's grasp.

In the grand design
Of life, every delay
Is a brushstroke, every
Pause a chance to
Reimagine the canvas.
As you navigate
through the
Shifts and turns, remember
That each moment of
Waiting contributes to the
Masterpiece
of your existence.

Not all delays hinder
Success;
Some bring hidden
Gifts wrapped in time's
Embrace.

Like the butterfly emerging
From its cocoon, delays
Transform our experience. They
Invite us to pause,
To breathe, and to
Appreciate the beauty of
The journey, not just
The destination. In every

Moment of waiting, there's
A chance to grow,
fluttering softly
Through life's moments.

The worth is
Not known if
We grasp too
Soon!
The value
Lies in waiting,
The dreams summed
In delays.

Worth the delay
Of night after
Day, worth the
Flower's bloom from
Bud. Patience paints
A brighter scene,
Unveiling life's hidden
Truths.

The sweetest fruits
Come from the
Wait, their flavors
Deepened by delays.
Lessons learned from
Life's pauses are
Treasures truly sublime.

Love, too, in
Its own time,
Finds its way
Into our hearts.
Though delayed, it's
Worth the wait,
Binding souls that
Won’t depart.

So embrace the
Journey’s pace, and
Let each moment
Unfold. For in
The heart of
Delays, lies a
Worth untold.

Every delayed
Gift is precious
And worth the wait!

Hey, little star,
Your twinkle shines brighter
After the pause, a
Delay that proves its
Worth!!!!

The On-Time Payment !!!

Unexpressed love,
Words left unsaid
At the crucial moment,
Will forever leave
A scar on the heart!

A "thank you"
Delivered in its
Rightful moment,
Holds immeasurable value,
Mending and uplifting.

A "sorry" offered
As soon as
The mistake is realized,
Heals wounds and
Restores trust.

Timely expressions of
Gratitude and regret
Are the true
Currency of the heart,
The on-time payment
That ensures bonds
Remain unbroken and
Love endures.

A "thank you"
Is a gentle rain,
Nourishing the soil,
Reviving the roots
Of a cherished bond,
Turning moments
Into lasting memories.

A "sorry" is a
Soft morning dew,
Cleansing the air,
Refreshing the spirit,
Bringing new light
To a shadowed day,
Restoring harmony’s glow.

In the quiet spaces,
Where words are few,
A sincere "thank you"
Lights the way,
Illuminating paths
In the dark,
With a warmth
That lingers.

The heartfelt "sorry"
Bridges gaps
Widened by silence,
Filling the void
With compassion's touch,
And weaving forgiveness
Into the fabric
Of relationships.

"Thank you" echoes
In the chambers
Of the heart,
Resonating like a
Melody of gratitude,
Each note a
Celebration of connection,
Each chord a
Recognition of kindness.

"Sorry" whispers
Through the corridors
Of regret,
A soft voice
In the storm,
Seeking to mend
The broken pieces,
And bring solace
To wounded hearts.

Together, "thank you"
And "sorry" form
A symphony of
Emotional currency,
A dance of
Acknowledgment and healing,
Creating a rhythm
That binds souls
In harmony.

The strength of
A "thank you"
Is in its simplicity,
A gesture of
Pure appreciation,
A bridge that
Spans the distance
Between hearts.

The depth of
A "sorry"
Is in its honesty,
A testament to
True remorse,
An offering of
Sincere contrition,
Healing the rifts
That time has
Widened.

These phrases,
Simple yet profound,
Carry the weight
Of our feelings,
Transforming moments
Into lasting ties,
And ensuring that
Love and respect
Remain steadfast.

Sorry and thank you,
Like the sun and the moon,
The universe's
Twinkling currency,
Makes our hearts rich.

Hey, little star,
The on-time twinkle,
The perfect happiness,
Makes you the
Twinkling star forever!

The Invisible Courier !

A random compliment
From a stranger's lips,
A soft smile from
A baby we pass,
A cheerful "hi" from
A child at play,
The pen lent by
A friend on a
Forgotten day.

The just-started lift
Stopped for you
By an unknown hand,
A door held open
In a crowded place,
A kind note slipped
Into your mailbox,
A warm meal shared
When you were hungry.

The comforting presence
Of a friend in need,
A gentle word of
Encouragement when you doubt,

An umbrella offered
On a rainy day,
A helping hand
When your burdens are heavy.

The quiet gestures
That go unnoticed,
A heartfelt smile from
A stranger in passing,
A shared laugh
With a new acquaintance,
The way someone listens
When you need to talk.

Exists an invisible courier,
Delivering gifts of love,
Wrapped in moments
Of unexpected kindness,
The unspoken bonds
That warm the heart,
A network of unseen
Affection connecting us.

Hey, little star,
Not all stars are visible—
Some are hidden
In the clouds,
Yet still twinkling,
Guiding others' smiles!!!

Out for Delivery !

Travelled through mountains,
Like the water
Carving paths,
Crossed the oceans,
Along with the birds,
Slapped the trees
With love,
Like the wind,
Chilled your cheek
With the cold breeze.

Danced over valleys,
Like the playful stream,
Touched the sun
In its radiant beam,
Cooled by the shadows,
Under ancient canopies,
Whispered through forests,
In gentle melodies.

Climbed to the peaks,
Where the air is thin,
Gazed at the stars,
With a hopeful grin,
Flew with the hawks,

In the crisp, high air,
Sailed through the clouds,
Without a single care.

Melted in the warmth
Of the first morning light,
Embraced the day's promise,
With the dawn's delight,
Drifted through the valleys,
In the soft mist,
Sought the quietude
In nature's gentle twist.

Through the lessons
Learned from pain,
Through the tears
Wetted the pillows,
Through the patience
Grew from the trials,
Found strength in the
Endless miles.

Glimpsed the horizon
In moments of despair,
Found solace in the
Quiet prayers,
Navigated the storms
With unwavering hope,
Discovered resilience
In the endless scope.

Found clarity
In the deepest night,
Embraced the struggles
With unwavering might,
Turned each setback
Into a guiding star,
Chose the path
To healing, however far.

Witnessed the beauty
In every small success,
Felt the joy
In the process,
Learned to cherish
Each fleeting moment,
Saw the light
In the silent foment.

Understood the worth
In every struggle faced,
Appreciated the growth
That patience traced,
Found the rewards
In every lesson learned,
Saw the value
In the love earned.

Like the butterfly
Out of the cocoon,
Like the pearl
Out of the shell,

Like the flower
Blooming from the bud,
Like the sun
Rising from the horizon,
Like the river
Breaking through the dam,
Like the dawn
Chasing away the night,
Like the flame
Igniting the dark.

Hey, little star!
And now it's out
For delivery,
Passing through all this
To twinkle better!

Hey, little star,
Evolved as superstar,
Enough of signature,
Just put the autograph
And receive the
Gift of life,
To twinkle better!!!!!!!!!!!!!

Complementary Gifts

The Unreceived Gift!

A little one prays for a tiny toy,
While God plans a life-sized teddy.
Eyes catch a happy child, an elderly pair,
But miss the fainting granny or a tragic fall.
You love the sweetness in your favorite soul,
Yet uncover their untold inhuman side.
Short, cute texts sent; the backspaced thoughts unsaid.
What's received and what's withheld,
What's seen and unseen,
Heard and unheard,
Known and unknown,
Experienced and unexperienced,
Blessed and seemingly unblessed—
Whatever and what-not,
Everything, in its own time, is a gift!
Everything is gifted, somehow, someway!!

The Unknown Gift!

The sea never knows how deep she is,
The sky never knows how high he is,
The dog never knows how gentle he is,
The cat never knows how cool she is,
The heart never knows how blessed it is,
And the mind never knows how unblessed it is!!

The Unrealised Gift!

The hunger behind the mom's "I am full!"
The sacrifice behind the dad's "I love my job!"
The longing behind the grandpa's "When will you come?"
The urge behind the granny's "What do you want to eat?"
The care behind a stranger's "Hey, your cloth."
The love behind a sibling’s fight,
The comfort behind a friend's joke,
Every "How are you?" and every "Have you reached or eaten?"
The gift behind every unrealised moment!!!

The Real Gift!

An innocent smile,
A sincere “sorry” spoken—
Time spent, “thank you" given!

The Court of Gift!

In the court of self,
Everyone argues the case—
Forgetting You are the sole judge!

It's you, who opened the window
It's you, who let the breeze inside!
It's you, who opened the door
It's you who let the storm!
It's you, who stood on shore!
It's you who should get wet!
It's you who wanted the view,
It's you who should climb!
It's you, who chose the path
It's you, who have to walk through!
It's you, who loved
It's you, who should get hurt!
It's you, who wanted to be strong,
It's you who should stay!

The Gift of Promise!

Some promises made
But never kept, and some never
Made, yet, kept forever!

The Metered Gift!

The kilometers become feet,
When the feet travel to embrace love.
The feet turn into meters,
When love is measured!

The Hidden Gift!

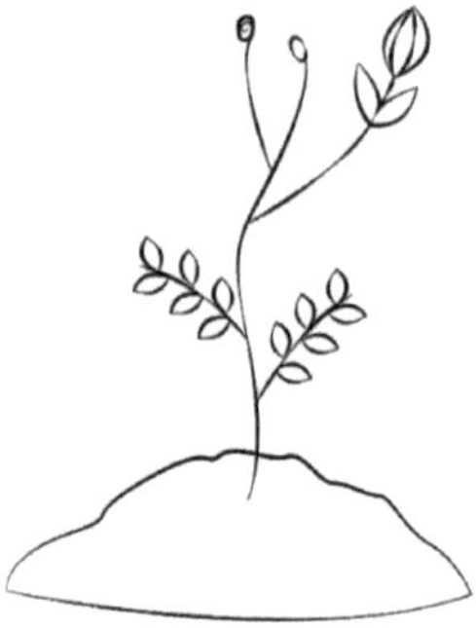

Eyes gaze upward to catch the tears,
Bathroom walls cradle the secret cries.
Running pipes roar louder than the painful screams,
Pillows and screens drenched in sorrow.
A gift was given to conceal the pain,
Yet this gift remains forever hidden!!!

Those Gifted Days!

The thrill of the last bell ringing after the final exam,
Signaling the start of vacation, and a trip to your favorite place!
Journeys that carry you into the heart of cherished memories,
With "One more story, please!" you beg Grandpa to tell.

The warmth of Grandma's cooking fills the air,
Her hands crafting your favorite dish with care.
Pillow fights and bike rides with your favorite uncle,
Laughter echoing like music through the breeze,
And those playful fights over who gets to play the best song.

Eagerly awaiting the day a new family member arrives,
As unconditional love blooms with the addition of a new relation.
Watching your cousin being born, then growing before your eyes.
Cuddling your sibling, like a doll brought to life!

The joy of spotting the store vehicle turn the corner,
Running barefoot, excitement alive in every step.
Saving coins in your pocket, each one a golden ticket,
To share a feast with street friends, like kings of the neighborhood.

Roaming with your favorite friends beneath wide-open skies,

Rented cycles squeaking with adventure,
Kitchen games where spoons became swords,
And tea parties that tasted like dreams served in tiny cups.

Weekend movies, treasure hunts on the screen,
Trips to the park that felt like stepping into a painting,
Family journeys that seemed boundless, as endless as the horizon.

Shopping for school supplies—crisp paper and fresh ink,
Crafts and art projects where your imagination soared.
Those favorite cartoons you waited all day to watch,
Lighting up the room—and your heart.

Those days, when your only duty was:
Wake up, get ready, play, sleep, and repeat.
Those days, when your only fear was:
"Oh no, I haven't started my holiday assignment!"
Those days, when your greatest worry was:
"Oh no, the holidays are nearing their end!"

Even after all these years,
That blush you feel when recalling those memories,
The nostalgic warmth as you rewatch old cartoons,
That sudden pause in your heart when you cross those familiar places,
As if time stands still for just a breath.

Even now, your mind weaves most of your dreams
With threads of childhood and schooldays,
Taking you back to the simplest joys ever lived.
You know, deep inside, it's those gifted days
That keep you moving forward, now and forever.

You never knew it back then, but now you realize—
Those days were the gifted days of your life!
And perhaps, just maybe, the life you're living now
Will one day become the gifted days you long to relive.
So live each moment fully—
Realize every moment you live, and truly live!

A Letter Gifted to the Hero of my Life!

To,
The Hero of My Life!

Like a beautiful poem,
Like a miraculous magic,
Like the dawn breaking through the night,
Like the gentle rain after a drought,
Like the light after darkness,
Like an unexpected blessing,
You came into my life.

Like a pillar of strength,
Like a cheerleader in my corner,
Like the foundation of my dreams,
Like the unwavering support
In every challenge I face,
Like the calm in every storm,
You stood with me.

Maybe some promises
Are meant to be broken,
But some promises
Are never made,
Yet kept forever!
Thanks for that promise
In my life,
For trying to be
The steadfast person
I rely on.

Many say soulmates are bound
Through every birth, every lifetime.
Ours felt like pure magic,
A masterpiece,
Written by God's own hand.

No one believes
The impossible coincidences in our story—
Unbelievable, even to us.

But that's the beauty of it,
Our love story is no ordinary tale,
It's a divine movie,
Directed by God Himself.

Lucky to have
The best friend
And life partner
In one,
Your love
Illuminates every page
Of my life.

Thank you
For everything,
Your love
Has brightened
Each and every page
Here!

Hey, little star!
You may be a little star,
But you are my superstar!
It may be a roller coaster,
But let's twinkle together!
Better and better,
Forever and ever!!!

With love,
Your Little Star!

A Letter Gifted to my Dad !

When the night knocks,
And darkness swirls, a soft whisper through the trees,
We leave our sweet little home
In the charming village,
To seek out my favorite creature—
Huge yet cloaked in shadows, tusks glowing.
While others fear its imposing might,
You, concerned, guide it gently back to its home,
And place your daughter in the backseat.
An adventurous ride unfolds,
Where excitement and joy travel side by side,
Granting thrilling moments!

Never spoken love, but memories always cherished:
Making my favorite meals together,
Holding up my socks so I can wear them easily,
Ironing my handkerchief,
Doing all the house chores,

Crafting with our hands the creative arts,
Fishing on weekends,
Midnight horror movies,
Dancing to mobile ringtones, ignoring the calls,

Holding snakes and capturing scorpions,
And letting them back to their home,
Safeguarding others,
Tales of adventures and bets.

Picking me up from just a street away,
Following the bus if I wished to travel alone,
Guarding me with unwavering strength,
Cooking for those in need,
Offering your meal to strangers, even when you have little,
Feeding street dogs within our home,
Aiding accidents with your little girl in tow,
Questioning wrongs,
Championing equality in every way!
Planting seeds of kindness from the start!
Growing courage from a tender age!

Feared by many,
Yet controlled only by your daughter.
Snakes or ghosts,
No fear when you are near.

And here I am,
Sharing our moments,
Lifetime memories,
Through every day of my life.

Not sure how many in the world are lucky enough
To parent their own parent—
The daughter becoming the father
And the father becoming the child,
Witnessing each other's growth.
The tragedy reversed our roles,
But the bond and memories remain the same!

A Letter to the Shero of My Life !

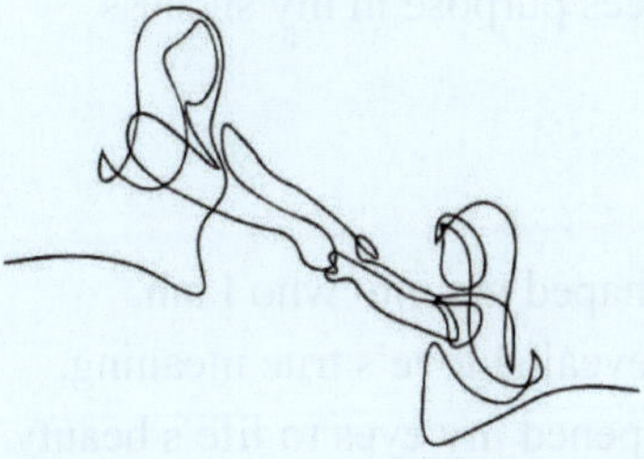

To,
The Shero of My Life

Disclaimer: This poem is a lengthy and steady tribute. It follows a consistent rhythm, reflecting the unchanging nature of a mother's love. Yet, in the end, the love for a mother gracefully accepts and embraces this flow.

sHE'RO
— the hero in my life.

She
— who is born for me,
— who gives her all,
— who sacrifices her dreams.

She
— who thinks of me every moment,
— who finds joy in my smile,
— who sees purpose in my success.

She
— who shaped me into who I am,
— who revealed love’s true meaning,
— who opened my eyes to life’s beauty.

She
— who guides me from the start,
— who holds my hand through every trial,
— who shows me the way forward.

She
— who spreads kindness everywhere,
— who inspires me endlessly,
— who believes in me without hesitation.

She
— who works tirelessly for my dreams,
— who supports me through every struggle,
— who always puts me first.

She
— who lives selflessly,
— who knows my heart's desires,
— who gives her love, patience, and strength.

She
— who faces every challenge with courage,
— who stands by me,
— who cherishes our moments together.

She
— who celebrates my achievements,
— who comforts me in sorrow,
— who guides me with wisdom.

She
— who taught me resilience and kindness,
— who showed me how to love,
— who revealed selflessness's beauty.

She
— who made sacrifices quietly,
— who gave without expecting anything back,
— who believed in my potential.

She
— who embraced my dreams as her own,
— who ensured my happiness,
— who cared for every need.

She
— who saw my potential when I couldn’t,
— who rejoiced in my successes,
— who supported me through failures.

She
— who makes my life beautiful,
— who brightens my days,
— who fills my world with love.

She
— who created cherished memories,
— who held me close when I faltered,
— who is my rock in hard times.

She
— who gives me strength,
— who demonstrates perseverance,
— who teaches me bravery.

She
— who is my anchor in storms,
— who makes every sacrifice seem small,
— who gives everything to see me happy.

She
— who loves me beyond words,
— who is the heart of our home,
— who makes sure I feel cherished.

She
— who is the light of my life,
— who shows me the beauty of selflessness,
— who makes me feel valued and special.

She
— who never thinks of buying even a saree
— while dolling me up as a princess,
— who runs tirelessly,
— holding up all the pains and strains.

She
— who always sees the best in me,
— who is my inspiration and guide,
— who helps me realize my potential.

She
— who stands by me unwaveringly,
— who makes every sacrifice worthwhile,
— who never stops loving me.

She
— who makes my life beautiful,
— who prioritizes me always,
— who shows me the true meaning of love.

She
— who is my greatest teacher,
— who never gave up on me,
— who taught me perseverance.

She
— who is my biggest supporter,
— who makes every challenge easier,
— who guides me with unwavering love.

She
— who makes every moment count,
— who shows me the power of kindness,
— who is my constant source of inspiration.

She
— who gives me strength when I need it most,
— who makes every day a gift,
— who loves me unconditionally.

She
— who is my everything,
— not just "she," but the s'HERO of my life.

Yes, when it comes to her,
It's all about only me!
I am her world,
Her life revolves around me.
Her heart beats every second for me!
When she lost the meaning of life,
She kept me as her dictionary,
Finding purpose through my existence!

From you,
I learned the meaning of love—
Not just love,
But unconditional love.
You've never been one to take,
Always the one to give.

No one could have survived
What you've been through,
Not even me.

I see Saraswati within you,
Illuminating the lives of countless students.
You are the Mahalakshmi,
Blessing our home, and so many in need.
Forever the Annapoorni,
Offering nourishment with grace.

The Mother Teresa in you,
Showers boundless love.
It's rare, so rare,
To find a soul who cares,
Who loves without ever
Asking anything in return!

I live this life
because of her unwavering sacrifices.
Every tear, every drop of sweat,
she sheds for me.

Without her, I am incomplete.

Even infinite words cannot convey
the depth of her love sacrifice.
Thank you,
For making me
A little super star!
And Sorry
that
I twinkle
By taking
The light from you!

Love you, my dear Shero.

With love,
Dhamini d/o Umarani Kandhavel

It Rains Because of Good Souls !

Its rain, the rain that blesses the earth and us—
but not in expectation of returns from us!
It's rare, the soul that showered—
only love and care to all,
and not in expectation of anything at all!

It's a blessing, the baby that's born
after being longed for, wished for the most.
It's a miracle, the little, fragile life that could fight,
even once born, for better health.
It's will, the baby's will, that made the baby!

It's common to have one cool kid in school,
but here, our hero is that one adored by all.
It's adorable to imagine how the parents raised
this child
with all their love and care.
It's early, so early, to learn the meaning of pain.

It's hard when a teen considers
their parents above their own wishes.
It struggled—the innocent soul struggled much,
to survive in this cruel world.
It tried—the passionate human tried their best,
but ended up running, like all the rest.

It longed—the heart longed for love,
but learned to sacrifice for all.
It cared—the pure heart cared for all,
even when no one cared back!

It flew—the little bird flew across nature,
as if the world were near its end.
It's sad that none understood
its journey, the bird's journey,
that was coming to an end.

It’s brutal, even when the smallest pain is hard
for the bird to bear,
yet it went through lots of pain and fights.
It’s breathtaking, to imagine the soul—
that longed to live—realizing its last moments.

It dreamed—the pure heart dreamed many,
and now, many wish
whatever happened was just a dream!

It’s sweet, to think of days we shared—
moments of laughter, plans made, and dreams.
It’s bitter, when reality hits, and we’re left here
with memories like shadows, slipping through.

It’s proud, to have such a pure heart as a friend!
It’s painful, to know he was the one and only,
the pure heart we had with us—and now, no
more.

It’s ironic: the place he visited most
were temples, trusted God more than all!
Maybe that’s why God wanted him nearby.

It’s comforting, to believe his soul is safe
in realms we cannot see—yet it’s hard,
knowing the world feels less bright without him here.

It’s silent, the nights where his laughter once rang,
it’s lonely, the places we’d meet, now dim and empty.
It’s strange, how life keeps moving—
as if the world didn’t pause when the soul was gone.

It’s haunting, the spaces left by his absence:
in every conversation, in every joke,
in every future he won’t be a part of.

It's hard hitting, when all the places we went together,
Asking us back where the other one is !
And where did you left !

It's beautiful, how his kindness touched us all,
and strange, how even strangers speak of him—
the one who loved, and gave, and believed in us all.

It's inspiring, the strength he showed through trials,
the courage he had to face the world alone.
It's humbling, how he loved with all his heart,
even when the world gave him reasons to turn away.

It's heartbreaking, how life could be so unfair,
that such a light should fade before it could shine fully.
It's questioning, the faith that we hold,
wondering why good souls must leave so soon.

It's human, to search for answers in the stars,
to wonder if he's watching from afar,
to hope he's free, unburdened, flying high—
as free as the dreams he once held close.

It’s reassuring, the way we feel his presence still,
in laughter, in warmth, in kindness shared.
It’s bittersweet, the memories we cling to,
knowing they’re all we have left of him.

It’s peaceful, to think his soul found rest,
but haunting, to know he’ll be missed every day.
It’s forever—the love, the lessons he left behind,
a legacy of purity, a reminder of grace.

It’s a promise, that we’ll carry him forward,
his kindness, his laughter, his love for all.
It’s a vow, to live in ways he would admire,
to honor the light he brought into our lives.

It’s endless, the pain of losing him,
yet endless too, the joy he brought to each day.
It’s a balance, this ache and this gratitude,
for having known him, for having loved him.

It rains, because of good souls—
and somewhere, his soul still showers us,
a gentle rain of memories and love,
falling softly, asking for nothing in return.

In loving memory of KarthikRajan,
Who remains in our hearts forever !

A Letter to the Lord !

Thank you for
Choosing me as
"Your Little Star!!!!!!!!"

9 789363 300637

Printed by Libri Plureos GmbH in Hamburg, Germany